LOVING
BETTER

God Bless you

LOVING
BETTER

SECRETS TO LIVING A FULFILLED LOVING LIFE.

VICTOR HICKSON, SR

CHANGE
PUBLICATIONS

This book and all other Change Publication™ books are available at Christian bookstores and distributors worldwide. To order products, or for any other correspondence:

CHANGE PUBLICATIONS™ USA

305.283.6817

Email: rev.VictorHickson@gmail.com

Or reach us on the Internet: www.changingyourdirection.org

ISBN 13: 978-1-0878-8205-5

ISBN 13 E-BOOK: 978-1-0879-2946-0

For Worldwide Distribution, Printed in the U.S.A.

Dedication

This book is dedicated to the Father, Son and the Holy Spirit.

Acknowledgments

Special thanks to:

My wife, Veronica Ann Cure Hickson who has been my great support through the process of making this book a reality;

My mother, Maggie Lou Harris who has been my hero and mentor;

My grandparents, Johnny B. Hickson, Ceola Hickson, DH Harris and Louise Harris;

My Uncles, John Hickson, Freddie McSears, Wayman Bannerman, Antonio Hickson, Wardell Hickson, and Larry Harris;

My Aunts, Ernestine Morley, Doris Arwater, Patricia Rivers, Dianne McSears, and Kathy Bannerman;

And to all Full Deliverance Baptist Church Family.

Contents

FORWARD

There are volumes of materials across the world today — some offer little or no help at all. Others are simply copied from the internet or different sources. The regurgitating effects due to lack of fresh ingredients have left people discouraged from digging deeper. There is a piggy-back syndrome that is sweeping through the nations: companies as well as individuals are mirroring each other and copying and pasting. Such scenarios are creating setbacks in many areas of life everywhere! The age of technology has made everything easily accessible thereby pushing back on the people's commitment to qualify and excellence. The ease of a microwave concept of life is stealing away the depth of intelligence that has helped past generations to carry their heavy loads.

We will not see real advancements unless we step ahead of the challenges of our time. The world is ready for something extraordinary — something absolutely groundbreaking to alleviate the pain and suffering of the people. A tough world is not a world devoid of love and caring. In fact, love is the foundation of life. Understanding the value of love and the sacrificial approach of showing love will help the societies to advance beyond the selfishness of the people. The concept of love was to address the core issues of societies and communities of people. The element of hate that has permeated the world is creating a different environment and atmosphere by tearing into the fabrics of life.

When love is taken out of the menu, we have wrong ingredients and the mixture is what is destroying the human life. Conscience and reason has become outdated and irrationality is a new societal trends today. One thing about foundation is that, it is the supporting pillar that holds everything together or the structure will start to fall apart. The importance of love cannot be understated because life hinges on the value. I have read Loving Better and I must agree that we must turn back to love — not only loving ourselves but also loving other people. The practical instructions outlined in Loving Better is a remedial prescription for those experiencing difficulties with loving others.

A commandment is not an opinion; therefore, we need to consider why loving others is mandatory. I believe there must be a benefit for us because the law is a reward system to encourage the people. Love adds such a unique value into a person's life, and where the character of love is found, men are rewarded for their sacrificial obedience. A selfish generation is a hopeless generation, so a society that is filled with hate, lacks self-defense. Love is part of immunity because you exchange your love and caring with others! The returns are what heals the societies or their wounds will continue to multiply. The simplicity of Loving Better creates the occasion to help you adjust quickly — and begin to learn how to love again even if you have failed the test before. It is like stepping into a coaching class! You need to give your whole attention to every detail in this instruction manual and prepare yourself to apply the methods in your personal life.

In His Love,
Dr. John King Hill
Author, Men of Purpose

PREFACE

Over the years, the LORD had spoken to me consistently about loving, nevertheless, it took some time before the work project began on Loving Better. As always with writing intensive material, the intricate details invested into making this book a reality was simply sacrificial. To put together the diagnosis of love and carefully separate the numerous ingredients that undermine the core fabrics of true love, the simplicity of the writing was intentional for the purpose of clarity and quick digestion.

The meats and bones were seasoned together to allow for deeper personal experiences. We are in a generation where love has been mistaken for what it is not! And we have to see through the veils of our societal dysfunction and make deliberate choices to love again. Love is for sale today and it is evident that we have made a wrong turn from where true love supposed to take us as a people. Because love is genuine there is no substitute for the reality of love and no matter how much we buy into attraction, the need for love will remain magnified.

Love is not a product of human ingenuity but a divine life — a higher standard of exchange between people. To indicate that love does carry equal weight with our feelings, a commandment is rule of law that must be followed. We are finding it more difficult today to love because we have followed our feelings instead of loving and the end result is a society filled with hate and self-satisfaction. From the biblical records of extraordinary sacrifices, love has always been selfless rather than selfish.

It is noteworthy to bring to our attention why the Creator made love mandatory for us. I believe that the beauty of love is realized in our expression of love toward others. When we are held back by our feelings, we restrain the power of love from releasing the ointment to infect people around us with loving-kindness. Our acts of love are like medications and the prescriptions are like discovering healing antidotes. Therefore, we must not shy away from loving one another and people generally.

Love has the potential to heal a broken society. Love has the power to save a wandering life. Love has the ingredients to cure deep wounds and hurts. Love can cause the trajectory of people's lives to shift dramatically. In fact, love is higher than all acts of given and receiving because love is embracing the nature of God so there is no motive behind the expression. It is living and exuding love towards all! This book has been written to help you generate the passion to love from the depth of your heart. It is my earnest desire that it serve as a blueprint — a help guide in reorganizing your life. As you go through every page, may your life become engulfed with the compassion to forgive others and to love even those who have offended or done you wrong.

Sincerely,
Victor Hickson, Sr.

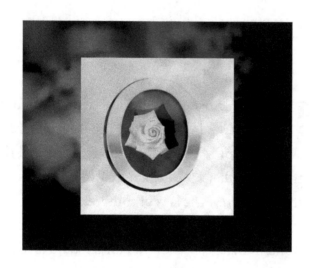

THE CONCEPT OF
LOVE

Most people use the word love without understanding the true meaning. Others use the word just for the fun of it, never thinking for a second that love is more than what they feel. Arguably, love is the most abused word in the dictionary. The lack of comprehension of what love really means explain the reason behind the dissolution of relationships and marriages. When you understand love critically, you will develop the capacity to sustain your relationships with less stress and struggles.

Some people define love as a strong feeling of affection for another person. In other words, love is simply what they feel for other people. However, if we consider how the Scriptures define love, it is much more than what people feel. Take, for example, the famous John 3:16 scripture, which says:

For God so loved the world, that he gave his only begotten Son, that whoever believes in him should not perish, but have everlasting life.

It is evident from the word of Apostle John that the love God has for the world is more than feelings. He did something practical as a result of His love—He gave His only begotten Son. True love does not end at feeling; it continues by taking action. Therefore, in addition to attraction and affection, love is expressed beyond feelings. There are actions in loving a person!

For example, a hired help will clean the house, do the ditches, wash clothes, and take care of the building without necessarily loving the boss. Another important part is that, it is realistically possible for a person to claim to have a strong feeling whether attraction or affection toward another person without doing anything practical to make his or her life better. Some people go as far as doing wrong things to those they claim to love like the case of a husband abusing the wife while confessing to love her deeply. Such an instance is a gross misrepresentations of love. Love is expressed with appropriate actions; there is a cooperation or linkage of benevolent deed.

Love can be triggered when two people meet and connect — some people refer to it as love at first sight. In this early stage, it can be described as friendships. As they spend more time together, they will begin to grow — mature and expand the connection through mutual interests. As they continue to develop by cultivating the relationship, they will start to discover each other's weaknesses and strengths. They will start to learn about how to forebear one another and overlook each other's flaws. This is the most critical part of love and it is at this point that many people fail the test of love. They do not seem to understand that love takes commitment and dedication besides tremendous sacrifices.

To summarize the concept of love, it is crucial to know that four major dimensions must be captured before you can conclude that you truly love a person.

The four dimensions are as follows:

1. Feeling
2. Action
3. Pleasure
4. Commitment

Therefore, to meaningfully state that you love a person, you must have a strong sense of attachment toward him or her. You must decisively act in ways that are consistent with how you feel towards him or her. You must derive joy in the activities you engage with him or her. And you must choose to be committed and dedicated to him or her regardless of his or her weaknesses and flaws. In 1 Corinthians 13:1–3, love is contrasted with some virtues, but the Apostle Paul says that love excels all.

Now, let us examine some of these virtues:

- Eloquence: The first verse of 1 Corinthians Chapter 13 states, Though I speak with the tongues of men and angels, and have not charity, I am become as sound-

i   tinkling cymbal. When Jesus Christ was
a.   he world, He commanded His disciples
to   world and preach the gospel to every creature (Mark 16:15). Besides the spiritual foundation of
this commission, this goal will take eloquence. To speak
eloquently is to communicate in ways that will appeal
to people, although we understand that the Holy Spirit
must convict the hearts of men. As crucial as this virtue
is to the accomplishment of the Great Commission, it
is useless without love. As such, love is more significant
and higher than eloquence!

- Prophecy: In the second verse of 1 Corinthians Chapter 13, the Apostle Paul says that even though a person
  possesses the gift of prophecy so much so that he or she
  understands all mysteries and knowledge, without love,
  the individual is as good as nothing. As we live in the
  world, we need daily guidance and comprehension of
  mysteries and hidden knowledge of God. Therefore, an
  individual who possesses the gift of prophecy is high-
  ly advantageous to others. However, the Apostle Paul
  makes it clear that without love, such a person would be
  nothing.

- Faith: In walking with God, faith is extremely important. In fact, without faith it is impossible to please God
  (Hebrews 11:6). It takes faith to know that there is a God
  and to accept the offer of His love in Jesus Christ. According to the Apostle Paul, faith is crucial for spiritual
  warfare. Christians are required to take the shield of

faith to quench all the fiery darts of the wicked (Ephesians 6:16). As important as faith is to the Christian life, Paul says in the second verse of 1 Corinthians Chapter 13 that though one has all faith, so as to remove mountains, without love the individual is nothing. In other words, love exceeds the spiritual weight of faith!

- **Charity:** God said in the Old Testament that the poor would not cease among the Israelites; as such, those who are rich are to help take care of the poor. In the New Testament as well, and even in contemporary times, we see that Christians take giving to the poor very seriously. Many groups of Christians have built schools, hospitals, orphanages, among other facilities, to help the poor and make life more enjoyable. Nevertheless, as important as charity may be, without love, it does not profit the person displaying that virtue. In other words, love is more significant than giving!

Characteristics of Love

From the teaching of Apostle Paul in 1 Corinthians Chapter 13:4–7, we learn that love has features that are visible and must be present before you can say it is true. The Bible said:

Charity suffers long, and is kind; charity envies not; charity brags not itself, is not puffed up, does not behave itself unseemly, seeks not her own, is not easily provoked, thinks no evil; rejoices not in iniquity, but rejoices in the truth; bears all things, believes all things, hopes all things, endures all things.

Let us dive into the details of these characteristics:

- Long-suffering: One who truly loves another person will be patient even when treated unjustly. It is not difficult to be patient when the person you claim to love is doing everything you desire right. However, true love express-es itself in suffering long and being patient with people even though they misunderstand your actions and mis-judge your intentions. Also, love manifests in being pa-tient with people while giving them enough time to ef-fect the change you want to see in their lives. You cannot truly claim to love a person when you give up too quickly on him or her.

- Kindness: One who possesses true love is compassion-ate and generous. He or she is also considerate and thoughtful of other people. Kindness means doing and saying the most excellent things to other people in the most pleasant ways. True love is not only kind when the recipients are behaving well. It remains kind even when misjudged and misunderstood. If you say you possess true love, but you are unkind, what you possess is not true love.

- Envies not: Any individual who possesses true love will not harbor a negative feeling toward other people be-cause they are more successful or have something they want. Some people can only demonstrate love to those whom they think have fewer abilities and possessions than them. When they see a person who has more material possessions, influence, and friends than them, they become jealous and envious. That is not a true love. True love will think and seek the good of all people irrespective of their social status, finances, or possessions.

- Humility: Love never boasts or brag arrogantly. It never seeks to win the praise of others people forcefully. It does not try to show off, and it is not hypocritical. It does not hold exaggerated ideas of its importance. If you possess true love, you will not be proud. One of the essential characteristics of true love is humility.

- Well-behaved: As mentioned previously, love is more than feelings; it must be expressed in deeds or actions. If you possess true love, you will behave well toward other people. Your character will be godly and lovely. Some notable unbelievers claim that they would have accepted the Christian teachings except for the character of some believers. Love is expressed in one's conduct; if you truly love, your behavior will be like Christ. It is very important to know that a dependable, quiet, consistent, and good character is the best way to advertise the Christian faith.

- Puts other people first: Those who possess true Christian love do not seek to have their own way. In other words, stubbornness and self-will are alien to love. When you possess the love of God, you think less of your rights and think more of what you are to do to make life better for other people around you. You are willing to set your rights aside if that is what is required to ensure that peace reigns.

- **Not provoked easily:** If you possess true love, you will not be ill-tempered. In other words, you will not flare up at the least incitement. You will know that all people have weaknesses, including you, and that the world itself is not perfect. Therefore, you make room for mistakes without getting annoyed. It is not that you will not be tempted with irritable feelings, but true love will keep those feelings in check.

- **Thinks no evil:** Some people routinely keep diaries: the daily records of other people's offenses. That's not a practice of a person who possesses true love. True love does not keep account of wrongs done by other people. It forgives and seeks to forget the wrongdoings of other people.

- **Rejoices not in iniquity:** The reaction of some Christians when another believer falters and falls into a public sin is horrifying. They respond as if they have just been waiting for the person to fail. But love does not rejoice when other people fail. People who possess true love weep when they hear a bad report about other people; in fact they mourn with broken heart. As much as true love does not excuse sin, it also forgives and protects the sinner. If you are always happy when other people go wrong, you do not possess true love.

Other important characteristics of love are listed as follows:

- It rejoices in the truth
- It bears trials and persecutions
- It believes God's words
- It is not quick to accept a bad report about other people
- It hopes that people and things will get better
- It remains strong amid sufferings

If you possess true love, these characteristics will be present in your life. However, if one or more characteristic is missing, you do not have to beat yourself down. There is always room for growth and expansion.

Types of Love

Since the times of the ancient Greeks, love has been a subject of study. From their ancient studies and in the Holy Scriptures, four primary types of love are identified:

1. Eros: This is also referred to as romantic love. Eros was the Greek god of love, sexual desire, physical love, attraction and affection. Promiscuity was the order of the day in the ancient Greek culture, and it was one of the most significant barriers that Apostle Paul had to tackle in his evangelistic outreaches in the Eastern Mediterranean. In the Bible, there is no mention of the word eros,

however, the Song of Solomon describes the passion of erotic (romantic) love. As Christians today, we are only permitted to display erotic love within the confines of marriage. In other words, only married couples are allowed to have sex with their partners. Therefore, erotic love is not to be demonstrated by all Christians outside the bounds of marriage.

2. **Storge:** This is the love between family members. It is the affection that grows between parents and children as well as siblings within a family. This is more like a natural love; in other words, you do not have to be a Christian to demonstrate this kind of love. Naturally, we are disposed to loving and protecting our family members. In the Bible, storge can be seen in the love of Abraham for Isaac, in Jacob's love for his sons, in the familial love of Mary, Martha, and Lazarus, among others. Also, the Bible enjoins believers to be devoted to one another with a brotherly love (Romans 12:10). The word translated as "be devoted" is the word philostorgos. As such, Christians all over the world, irrespective of race, color, or tribe are supposed to relate as family members bought into the family of God by the blood of Jesus Christ. So the next time you see another believer, think of them as one of your family members, because, indeed, they are your family member.

3. **Philia:** This is the kind of love that exists between friends. It is also the type of brotherly love that most Christians practice toward one another. Of all the types of love,

philia is the most common type found in the Scriptures. It has to do with care, honor, and compassion for people who have needs. It can also be described as an encompassing love for others. Jesus says, By this shall all men know that you are my disciples, if you have love one to another (John 13:35). The love described as an identifier of the Christian here is philia. Therefore, Christians are supposed to love one another and share an emotional bond as friends.

4. **Agape:** This is the highest form of love ever known—the love of God to man. It is immeasurable, incomparable, invaluable, priceless, and unbelievable. Agape is the divine nature of God, which is devoid of weakness and imperfections. Agape love is pure, unconditional, sacrificial, and perfect. This love is demonstrated in the substitutionary sacrifice of Jesus Christ, the only begotten Son of the Father, for our sins. It is noteworthy that after the resurrection of Jesus Christ, when He asked Peter if he loved (agape) Him, Peter replied that he loved (phileo) Jesus (John 21:15–17). This is probably the reason Jesus asked him three times. Without the Holy Spirit, it is impossible to possess or demonstrate agape love.

The Rationale for Love

If we want to be successful at accomplishing any task, we must first know the justification or rationale for committing to the task. In other words, if you do not see the reason to pursue the goal, it is most likely that you will not achieve it. There is a psychological and business mantra that reads "start with the why." The idea here is that your motivation for achieving a set purpose must come from your knowledge of the reason for that purpose. If you perceive the why as essential, you will not see the how as awkward or too demanding.

Imagine that there are two students at a university: one of the two knows that at the end of four years, he or she will be awarded a degree with which he/she can get an excellent job and be able to live a better life. The other student is mainly there to party without any expectation of what a degree might do for him or her. The most probable result will be that the latter will complain that the tasks required to meet the academic goal. He or she may see the requirements as too tedious, even though he/she may possess the ability to accomplish the task. However, the one who knows the why will focus on the end goal and carefully complete the requirements. If you know why you should love better, you will not think of the process as an impossible mission. The greatest justification for loving better is that God loves us first. This is clearly written in 1 John 4:11, Beloved, if God so loved us, we ought also to love one another.

If God, who is perfect, flawless, and supreme, loved us when we were unworthy of His love, it befits us to love our fellow human beings even though we may consider them unworthy of our love. In spite of our continual mistakes and flaws, God continues to love us. It behooves us as well to continue to love other people despite their weaknesses. Loving others is how we show gratitude to God for His unconditional love for us.

Another justification for us to love better is the fact that love is the only way through which we can have an intimate relationship with God. It is by loving Him and other people that we can truly make God happy and reciprocate His love toward us. All the law is summarized in loving God and our neighbors. If you think about this, you should not find it difficult to display the God-kind of love to other people, even when you consider them undeserving of love.

Benefits of Love

1. Through the love of God, we are freed from the power of sin and death.
2. Through the love of God, we are called the children of God, and only as such, can we enjoy all the benefits inherent in His great and precious promises.

Several advantages come as a result of loving God, loving ourselves, and loving our neighbors — other people generally. Love brings us the peace and joy we desire in life. Love helps us to become more aware of the plan of God for us and to accomplish the goal. Love helps us in witnessing to those who have not put their faith in Jesus Christ at the moment, and love makes the world to see us as true children of God.

In the next chapters, we will venture into how to love Christ, how to love yourself, how to love love your neighbors, and how to forgive others.

"Christian love, or agape love (God's love), is an unconditional love that is always giving and does not change whether the love given is returned or not. It devotes a total commitment of the heart to seek the other person's highest good no matter how they may respond."

T. D. Jakes

VICTOR HICKSON SR

NOTE

LOVING JESUS
CHRIST

The New Testament laid particular emphasizes on the believers loving Jesus Christ above all else. The love for the LORD is not something that stands aloof; it rests solidly on the love of Jesus Christ for the human race. This is to say that we are expected to love Him because He first loved us. The Apostle Paul shows us the link between the love for Jesus Christ and our conducts in 2 Corinthians 5:14–15, the Bible said:

For the love of Christ constrains us; because we thus judge that if one died for all, then were all dead: and that he died for all, that they which live should not from now on live to themselves, but to him which died for them, and rose again.

In 1 Corinthians 13:8–13, Paul also speaks of the love for Jesus Christ as that critical element that makes it possible to have a personal communion with God. And he places so much emphasis on the love of Jesus Christ in Romans 8:35–37, he concluded that not even persecution, famine, tribulation, nakedness, peril, sword, or even death can separate him from the love of Christ. If love for Jesus Christ is this crucial to the Christian life, it is expedient that we consider it critically.

Many people claim to love Jesus Christ, however, they do not lead their lives by that profession. Some think that love for Jesus Christ only means going to a Church building on Sunday for fellowship. In essence, there are several misconceptions about true Christian love for Jesus Christ. To set the record straight, we must now consider what love for Jesus Christ truly means.

What Does it Mean to Love Jesus Christ

To love Jesus Christ is to receive Him. No one can claim to love Jesus Christ who has not received His offer of salvation and forgiveness of sins. The very first step to loving Jesus Christ is accepting Him as Savior and LORD. John 1:11–12 states:

He came to his own, and his own received him not. But as many as received him, to them gave he power to become the sons of God, even to them that believe on his name.

The natural man is hostile toward the LORD — he/she does not want to have anything to do with Jesus Christ, and as such, cannot have the capacity to love Him. However, when the Holy Spirit regenerates a person, that individual's disposition toward the LORD begins to change. The Holy Spirit removes the heart of stone from those who accept Jesus Christ and gives them the hearts of flesh. Essentially, the Holy Spirit makes him or her a new creature. (See Ezekiel 36:25–27; 2 Corinthians 5:17–18).

If you are reading this material and you do not know how to receive Jesus Christ, it is straightforward and easy. You do not have to leave where you are at the moment. You do not have to pay any amount of money to anyone. All you need to do is accept your sinfulness, believe the Scriptures that Jesus Christ died for your sins and was raised up for your justification, and then ask Him in prayer to forgive your sins and make you a new creature. If you do this, the Holy Spirit will immediately come into you and perform that work; you will become a new creature instantly. It really does not matter how much wrong you have done before this time; Jesus Christ saves even the vilest of sinners.

To love Jesus Christ is to esteem Him higher than every other person or things (Luke 14:26; 16:13). Anyone who claims to love Jesus Christ must treasure Him more than anyone and anything. That individual must be willing to lay down everything, including his or her life in service to Him. To love Jesus Christ means that your most important purpose in life is living for Him, while your greatest joy is to be in His presence. Many people do not like this part of their love for Christ. But if you consider what Christ did for you, in that He left His glory in heaven, came to this world, gave His life for your sins to be forgiven and for you to have eternal life, then, you should not find it difficult to live in absolute surrender to Him.

To love Jesus Christ is to obey His instructions. Jesus says, If a man loves me, he will keep my words (John 14:23). If you do not obey the words of Jesus Christ, you simply do not love Him. Now, some of us have read through the Old and New Testaments, and we have seen several instructions, and we think, *But how can anyone fulfill all these commandments?* I am glad to tell you that the commands of Jesus Christ are not burdensome but light (1 John 5:3). This is so because when He gives you an instruction, He also gives you the ability to follow the instruction. In the New Testament, the Holy Spirit is given to us so we can obey the LORD. By taking heed to the teachings of Jesus Christ, we demonstrate our love for Him.

To love Jesus Christ is to think about Him always — to desire to hear about Him and to hear from Him. You must read about Him! You must seek to please Him! You must choose to be with His friends! You must desire to talk to Him in prayers! You must devote your time to talk to other people about Him! Finally, you must prepare to be with Him eternally! To say, I love Jesus Christ is not enough; the attributes and characteristics described above must show through us if we genuinely love Him with all our lives.

Why Should You Love Jesus Christ

As stated in Chapter One, if you do not know why you have to do something, you will consider that thing difficult, burdensome, or altogether impossible. The very first reason why we should love Jesus Christ is that He died for our sins. John 15:13 says, *Greater love has no man than this, that a man lay down his life for his friends.* If Jesus Christ did this much for us, then, we are to demonstratively reciprocate — show our love for Him. The Apostle John said, We love him, because he first loved us (1 John 4:19).

A Christian is expected to love Jesus Christ because the nature of the believer is love. The Holy Spirit has shed the love of God broadly in the hearts of the Christians (Romans 5:5). It is only natural for the believer to demonstrate his or her love for Jesus Christ. Christians should love Jesus Christ because it is the only way to grow and become more like Him.

Now that we have defined what it means to love Jesus Christ and the basis for loving Him, we will take the step further to discuss more on how to love Him even better!

How to Love Jesus Christ Better

1. Receive Him as your LORD and Savior: As I noted previously, it is impossible to love Jesus Christ without accepting His provision for the forgiveness of your sins. Even though you may go to Church and work diligently perhaps as a musician, protocol officer, among others, you cannot love Him if you do not have His Spirit. In other words, if you are not born again — born of the Spirit, you cannot love Jesus Christ at all. To be born again, you have to accept that you are a sinner and believe that Jesus Christ died in your place; then ask Him in prayer to forgive you of your sins and make you a new creature. This is the first step to loving Jesus Christ better.

2. **Meditate on His Words:** The LORD commanded Joshua, This book of the law shall not depart out of your mouth; but you shall meditate therein day and night, that you may observe to do according to all that is written therein: for then you shall make your way prosperous, and then you shall have good success (Joshua 1:8). If you want to develop the capacity to follow the instructions of Jesus Christ, you must know His Words: you must learn to meditate on His Words always. Think about what He has done for you from time to time and ruminate on His promises and commands. Set time apart every day just to meditate on the Words of the LORD. You can also write down some of the instructions of Jesus Christ from the Scriptures and place them in specific locations where you will see them consistently. Furthermore, it is profitable to purchase audio versions of the Bible and listen to them in your car or at home so you are constantly reminded of Him — His love for you, and your duties toward Him.

3. **Study about Jesus Christ:** The Scriptures have been given to us to know more about Jesus Christ. Therefore, to love Jesus Christ better, you must read His Words and study the Scriptures deliberately. Some people read and study the Scriptures only when they have free time, but a Christian who desires to love Jesus Christ better will set aside time to read and study the Scriptures including other Christian materials. While Apostle Paul was addressing the Colossians, he encouraged them by say-

ing, let the word of Christ dwell in you richly (Colossians 3:16). There is no way the Word of Christ can dwell richly in you if you do not give your time to read and study the written Words. It is important that you see the Word of God as your spiritual food. If you desire to grow physically, you know you must eat. In fact, you must maintain a healthy diet! Likewise, if you want to improve your love for Jesus Christ, you have to feed on His Words. You must treasure your Bible because therein you will find all the promises of God for your life.

4. **Pray to love Jesus Christ better:** Jesus Christ hears and answers our prayers! The Bible said, If you ask anything in my name, I will do it (John 14:14). He also assures us that the Father will give good things to those who ask Him (Matthew 7:11). There is nothing as good as loving Jesus Christ better. So we have the assurance that when we pray to love Him better, the Father will hear and answer us. To love Jesus Christ better should be our daily prayers. In Ephesians 3:19. the Apostle Paul prays that the Church will know the love of Jesus Christ, which exceeds all knowledge, and that they might be filled with all the fullness of God. Therefore, everyone who desires to love Jesus Christ better must learn to spend time in prayers to God for an increase in capacity to love Him better.

5. **Have faith in Christ:** The Writer of Hebrews says that without faith it is impossible to please God (Hebrews 11:6). When we pray to God to love Jesus Christ better,

we must believe that He has heard and answered us. It is impossible to love Jesus Christ without faith because it is only by faith that we grow to know Him. If your faith is weak, your love for Him will also be weak. And if your faith is strong, your love for Him will be actively strong. You must choose to believe what you read in the Bible about Jesus Christ. Secondly, you must ask the Holy Spirit to help you to grow in your love for Him and to walk in love.

6. **Be filled with the Spirit:** According to Romans 5:5, the love of God is shed broadly in our hearts by the Holy Spirit. This means that when you are filled with the Holy Spirit, you are equally filled with love for Jesus Christ. Jesus Himself said the Holy Spirit would guide us into all truth; of which, loving Him better is inclusive. The Writer of the book of Jude says, But you, beloved, building up yourselves on your most holy faith, praying in the Holy Ghost, keep yourselves in the love of God, looking for the mercy of our Lord Jesus Christ to eternal life (Jude 1:20–21). From these Scriptures, it is evident that one way to love Jesus Christ better is to pray in the Holy Spirit. When we are filled with the Holy Spirit and pray in the Holy Spirit, we increase our capacity to love Jesus Christ better and demonstrate our love for Him even in the midst of cruel persecutions and severe temptations.

7. **Obey Him:** It is vital that we make the point absolutely clear that the Holy Spirit empowers us to obey the words of Jesus Christ. The Bible said, For it is God which works

in you both to will and to do of his good pleasure (Philippians 2:13). We should all agree that the Holy Spirit helps us to obey the LORD. Nevertheless, we must never forget that we have to make the choice whether to follow Jesus Christ or not, in different situations or circumstances. It is important to know that every Christian can obey Jesus Christ without failing through the help of the Holy Spirit. The Holy Spirit is faithful. Always, your will is involved in obeying the LORD. This is the reason why different Christians obey Jesus Christ differently in their respective walks or relationships with Him. If you want to love Jesus Christ better by demonstrating that love in obedience, you must make the decision that no matter what happens, you will follow through on your decision to obey Him. You must choose to hate sin and all that it offers. You must flee from all unrighteousness and the works of the flesh. You must be sure to lead your life in a way that you do not make provisions for the flesh and to fulfill the lusts thereof. Some people think that all there is to loving Jesus Christ better is the Holy Spirit making all the decisions. They spend great time in prayers, but they do not actively resist sin or avoid all appearances of evil. In a long run, they will start to make excuses for sin by claiming that they are too weak. To be sincere, if you truly desire to love Jesus Christ better, your must be fully involved and engaged with the Holy Spirit.

8. Keep friends that love Jesus Christ: There is an adage or old saying, "Show me your friend, and I will tell you who

you are." It has been discovered that you are the average of five of your friends. In other words, if we take a critical look at five of your friends, we can describe who you are. Your friends will have a significant impact on you; therefore, you must choose friends who love Jesus Christ and make efforts to love Him better daily. If you keep friends who always discourage or attempt to dissuade you from obeying the LORD whether you are in a stressful situation or not, soon or later, your love for Jesus Christ will start to wax cold. On the other hand, if you keep friends who encourage and pray for you when you are faced with difficult challenges, your love for Jesus Christ will continue grow even stronger and stronger. I want to add one more important thing here, it is essential to join yourself with a fellowship of the Saints — an active members of a local Church and be accountable to a qualified Leader. By following this directive, you will keep yourself in check and have others watch over you when your love for Jesus Christ starts to waver or shake!

Loving Jesus Christ better has several benefits that includes but not limited to peace of mind, answers to prayers, more assurance of God's love, and better witnessing to others, and much more. My last point for you is that regardless of your level of love for Jesus Christ today, you can always grow to love Him even better. Therefore, do not give up on your endeavors or quit your efforts! Do not compare yourself with any other person. Continue to seek after Him and to love Him better everyday!

"You cannot give away something you don't have in you. How can someone love another person if they don't love themselves? We all need to accept ourselves—our personalities and imperfections—knowing that although we are not where we need to be, we are making progress. God wants us to love ourselves and our identity in Him."

Joyce Meyer

NOTE

VICTOR HICKSON SR

HOW TO LOVE YOURSELF

I n today's society, especially among the Christians, many people consider loving themselves an abomination — they mistake or misplace the connotation with selfishness instead of self maintenance and wellness. They simply believe that if they love themselves, they will go against God's commandment, which says to love Him first and love our neighbors second. However, in this Chapter, we will examine and dissect the difference between narcissism and true self-love, the justification for self-love, the benefits of loving yourself, and how to practice true self-love!

True Self-Love and Narcissism

It is very important that we learn to love ourselves as individuals. Jesus says the second commandment is to love your neighbor as yourself (Matthew 22:39). You must love yourself, but there's a limit to this love. If we are not careful, true self-love can degenerate into narcissism.

True self-love is an unapologetic decision to accept yourself, put yourself first, and demonstrate healthy self-esteem. True self-love is not anti-Christ, instead it stems from accepting who you are in Christ and displaying the confidence that befits such knowledge. When Jesus Christ was on earth, He practiced true self-love by setting time apart to rest, eat, and pray. He had times to attend to others, but He also had time to attend to Himself. He knew who He was, and the misrepresentation of His person by the people around Him did not deter Him. He spoke about Himself confidently, however, He never placed Himself above God. This is true self-love.

Narcissism, on the other hand, is a personality disorder that makes a person have an exaggerated sense of self-importance and a complete lack of compassion. Narcissists believe that they are superior to others, and that it is only a few people who are special like them who can comprehend them. They are always seeking validation from people around them.

There are vast differences between true self-love and narcissism and here are some of the differences:

1. **Need for recognition**: *People who practice true self-love have high self-esteem; as such, they do not need anyone to validate them. They do not seek to make themselves known in ways that are not reasonable, and they do not need people to congratulate them for their achievements. They are aware of their goals and the reasons behind those goals, and the satisfaction they derive from achieving their goals brings them happiness. If anyone*

acknowledges the achievement of these goals, it is okay by them; but if no one notices, it does not diminish their joy. On the other hand, narcissists do not think they are successful if there is nobody around to witness their successes or congratulate them. If anyone does not praise them for what they have done, they will not consider that endeavor a successful one. The only thing that truly satisfies them is the admiration and approval of others. In this case, whether they have done well or not is not the focus; they focus mainly on the praises of men.

2. **Accepting weaknesses**: *People who love themselves admit that they have weaknesses and flaws and do everything within their power to improve on those weaknesses. They do not excuse their flaws, nevertheless, they do not hide their faces because of them. They are aware that every human being has weaknesses and flaws and that we are all works in progress. Narcissists, on the other hand, try to do everything within their power to cover up their defects; they are hypocritical and pretentious. They do not mind even giving bribes and telling lies to cover up their sins. If anyone ever tries to point out a weakness to them, they think the individual either hates them, wants to pull them down, or has a misconception about them. They feel that they are perfect in every way!*

3. **Self-Acceptance:** *Individuals who practice true self-love know who they are and accept who they are. They accept their body size, shape, tribe, color, and race. They are comfortable being themselves and are confident about what they can offer. This does not mean that they are satisfied with sin or any bad habit; instead, it means that they are convinced of their per-*

sonality. They see themselves as creations of the Almighty God, and they know that it is only His Words about them that truly matters. As such, they do not seek to make profound changes in their lives just to please other people and be in their good books. Their happiness is derived from the LORD, and not from men. Narcissists, however, are not anything like that. They are often very greedy and lack contentment. They always fantasize about an ideal life. They are never satisfied with their body size, shape, color, tribe, or race. They believe that they deserve a better life than they are living currently, but they never have a sense of satisfaction when their life improves.

4. **Humility and empathy**: *People who have true self-love are generally humble and empathetic — they are compassionate! They do not judge other people wrongfully because they know they make mistakes as well. They think good of other people because they are comfortable with themselves. They are so secure in themselves that the achievements of other people do not move them to jealousy or envy. As such, they support and encourage other people to do better in life. They know that they have a unique purpose from God to achieve and that no one can take their places. Therefore, they motivate and inspire other people to seek their unique goals and fulfill them too. Narcissists cannot bear with the prosperity of other people. When other people succeed, they become sad and withdrawn. They seek ways to undermine their achievements so they can feel they are ahead of them. They never motivate other people to succeed unless they know that the person cannot do better than they have done. If anyone comes to them for counsel, they will discourage the per-*

son if they know that his or her accomplishments will outshine theirs. They like to be seen as the most successful, most prosperous, and most prominent. They are never genuinely concerned about other people; at best, they can only fake to be concerned. They are mostly satisfied when people depend and look up to them.

5. **Esteeming and appreciating others:** *Individuals who have true self-love esteem and appreciate other people for the goodness they do. They know that they cannot achieve all the goals on earth by themselves. For that reason, they appreciate the contribution of other people to the general well-being. They do not make anyone feel as though they are a waste or that they are not useful. These people make good friends because they are extremely supportive. They also know and do what it takes to make other people function to their highest capacity. On the other hand, narcissists do not value other people. They think that they can achieve all things by themselves and that what other people achieve is not significant. The only time they see other people as valuable is when they intend to use those people for their benefits. The only person whom the narcissist feels is valuable is another narcissist like him or herself.*

6. **Competition with peers:** *People who have true self-love do not compete with other people. Rather than compete, they run their own race and compete with themselves. They aim to become better today than they were yesterday. They do see other people as a threat; instead, they see them also as trying to become better and achieve happiness. They are confident of the fact that satisfaction is not a limited resource. For the fact that*

someone else is happy does not hinder their joy in any way. They do not see any sense in competing with their peers whether for attention, recognition, or opportunities, etc. Narcissists, however, are always in competition with other people. They must be doing either better or pretend to be doing better. They are happy only when they can dominate and manipulate other people. If anyone seems to outshine them, they become unhappy. They have to be the center of attraction and want others to worship them. They cannot relate with other people effectively because they will always seek for ways to pull those people down.

From the preceding, it is evident that true self-love and narcissism are polar opposites. While every Christian is expected to have true self-love, no narcissist can successfully obey the Christian faith. The big question is, why must Christians practice true self-love?

Justification for the Practice of True Self-Love

In Matthew 22:36–40, the Bible said:

Master, which is the great commandment in the law? Jesus said to him, You shall love the Lord your God with all your heart, and with all your soul, and with all your mind. This is the first and great commandment. And the second is like to it; you shall love your neighbor as yourself. On these two commandments hang all the law and the prophets.

Here we see Jesus Christ reiterating that the second great-est commandment is to love your neighbor as yourself. This is the very reason why Christians should practice self-love. If we are required to love other people as ourselves, we must love ourselves. If we do not love ourselves, we cannot love other people effectively. For instance, if you are always doubtful of your abilities, you will also doubt the skills of other people. If you are critical of yourself, you will be critical of other people. If you accept your weaknesses and flaws, you will also ac-cept the shortcomings and deficiencies of others as well. If you believe in yourself, you will also believe in other people. This is the reason why Christians need to learn to practice true self-love!

Benefits of Loving Yourself

People who love themselves do the following and enjoy the benefits.

a. They do not compare themselves with other people, and neither do they engage in self-made competition. As a result, they are consistently happy. Because they are happy, they have decreased risk of health issues, such as depression, hypertension, anxiety, heart at-tacks, among others. They also have a boosted im-mune system.

b. They accept what they cannot change, and work on what they can change. For that reason, they channel their energies in the right direction and achieve greater things.

c. They readily delegate tasks to other people, and they are better team leaders, and their teams produce more.

d. They allow everyone around them to grow. These later become helpful to them because of the growth and development that they have experienced.

e. They are not deterred by the misrepresentation and misconception of other people about them. As a result, they do the will of God, even in stressful situations.

f. They accept their weaknesses and flaws and the shortcomings of other people. Therefore, they are less judgmental and critical so, they are able to help groom more people toward perfection.

How to Practice True Self-Love

Here are some principles that can guide you in practicing true self-love so that you do not end up being a narcissist:

- **Do not place too much emphasis on your external attributes:** *True self-love involves being self-aware. In other words, you know your weaknesses and your strength, and you know that your physical characteristics do not determine who you are. Therefore, always place a premium on who you truly are rather than who other people perceive you to be. Never try to* *impress anyone. Allow people to correct you rather than be a hypocrite. Work on your weaknesses every day and make sure you become better.*

- **Never compare yourself with another person:** *Never set your goals based on efforts to achieve more than other people. Think about your purpose for existence — find out what God wants you to do in life, and prioritize your efforts on how to move forward towards achieving that goal. Be content with the material possessions you have while you work harder and smarter to meet your other needs. Do not allow the desire for material possessions to diminish your relationship with the LORD and your family members. Work legally and honestly and depend on the LORD to bless and prosper you.*

- **Forgive yourself always:** *Sometimes when we do what we know is wrong, we pray and ask God to forgives us, but we continue to blame ourselves afterward. Never be so concerned about what people think about you that you fail to forgive yourself when you make a mistake. It is crucial that you accept the fact that you cannot change what happened in the past. However, you can alter the way you feel about what happened, and you can prevent it from happening again. You should see your past failures and mistakes as opportunities to learn from them and become better. Therefore, own your mistakes, forgive yourself, and move on with your life.*

- **Love and accept yourself:** *To practice true self-love, you have to love your body shape and size, color, race, and tribe. Some people are too concerned about what other people think about* *their body. The truth is that if you are slim, there are people who will not like you. On the other hand, if you are chubby, there are people who will not like you. Do not spend all your time trying to add weight or reduce weight; albeit, stay healthy.*

- **Be kind to yourself:** *Several people know how to be kind to every other person than themselves. Dear reader, you have to be kind to yourself. Do not allow evil thoughts about yourself to grow in your heart. If you know you cannot say what you think about yourself to a loyal friend, then stop the thought. Think of yourself kindly, talk to yourself kindly, and rebuke yourself kindly. Take yourself to the right places and enjoy life once in a while when you have the means. Wear suitable clothes and use good things. However, never allow the love of money and material possession to take hold of you. Always remember that your material possessions does not define you. You are defined by what God says about you.*

- **Express and invest in yourself:** *Be free to express yourself in whatever way you choose, as long as it does not contradict the laws of God, the laws of the nation and it does not hurt other people. Do the things that make you happy: visit places that make you happy, and relate with people who make you happy. Also, you have to think about growing yourself. Do not concentrate your whole effort on developing other people that you leave yourself out. Buy and read books that develop you, attend seminars and conferences. In short, do the things that will make you better today than you were yesterday.*

- **Surround yourself with people who make you happy:** *Some people are so afraid of losing people that they keep toxic* *people in their lives. There is nobody who is absolutely indispensable to your well-being except God and you. Therefore, do not allow toxic people or relationships to remain in your life. Separate from them and keep only friends that help move you forward.*

Remember that you are to love your neighbors as you love yourself; therefore, begin to love yourself today so that you can love your neighbors the same way.

"Love as distinct from "being in love" is not merely a feeling. It is a deep unity, maintained by the will and deliberately strengthened by habit; reinforced by the grace which both partners ask, and receive from God. They can have this love for each other even at those moments when they do not like each other; as you love yourself even when you do not like yourself."

C. S. Lewis

NOTE

HOW TO LOVE
OTHER PEOPLE

J esus says, Everyone will know by this that you are my disciples—if you have love for one another (John 13:35). By
this powerful statement, He did something very unique:
He formed a group of people that will be identified only by
their love for other people. There are thousands of groups in
the world, and they are known in different ways. Some groups
are recognized by skin colors, some by dress codes, some by
trainings, and others by beliefs, etc. However, Jesus formed
a group where neither skin color nor social status matters
except love. They are solemnly identified by love for other
people. This group is what we generally refer to as Christians.
Therefore, if you consider yourself to be a Christian, please
take this Chapter extremely serious!

What Does It Mean to Love Other People?

When we talk about loving other people, it does not mean
falling in love with everybody. In other words, loving other
people does not mean having a romantic relationship with

every individual you meet. It also does not mean keeping everyone as close friends. Here is what it really means to love other people:

- **Acting with compassion**: *Jesus' story of the good Samaritan in Luke 10:30–37, implied that he who showed compassion is the one who loved his neighbor. Compassion does not stop at just feeling bad or sorrowful for the situations of other people. Compassion does something rather than being passive! It attempts to address the need. It is written, As Jesus got out, he saw the large crowd, and he had compassion on them and healed their sick (Matthew 14:14). In another situation, it says, Then Jesus called the disciples and said, I have compassion on the crowd because they have already been here with me three days and they have nothing to eat. I don't want to send them away hungry since they may faint on the way. The disciples said to him, Where can we get enough bread in this desolate place to satisfy so great a crowd? Jesus said to them, How many loaves do you have? They replied, Seven, and a few small fish. After instructing the crowd to sit down on the ground, he took the seven loaves and the fish, and after giving thanks, he broke them and began giving them to the disciples, who then gave them to the crowds. They all ate and were satisfied, and they picked up the broken pieces left over, seven baskets full. Not counting children and women, there were four thousand men who ate (Matthew 15:32–38). It is evident from these scriptural verses that if you are filled with compassion, you will also act* *in ways that correspond to that feeling. You cannot claim to have compassion on other people and sit idly while they suffer needs that you can provide for. Therefore, loving other people is acting in ways that demonstrate that you have compassion and care for them. You provide for their needs, you accommodate or house them, and you visit them when they are sick besides other acts of kindness. Loving other people is helping them to live good lives to the full extent of your ability or capacity.*

- **Being observant:** *The Apostle Paul told the Christians in Philippi that each of you should be concerned not only about your own interests, but about the interests of others as well (Philippians 2:4). Loving other people involves being concerned about their well-being, however, this cannot be done without being observant. This is because some people will not tell you that they have problems. Loving them requires for you to observe their facial expressions, appearances, or asking questions to make sure they are doing okay. You cannot claim to love other people when you do not observe anything about them that will create the occasion for you to show your love for them.*

- **Speaking kindly:** *Loving other people will help you to avoid pulling them down with your words instead of building them up. It involves speaking words of encouragement to those who are down, praising those who have done well, and speaking more about the good in people's lives than their negatives. When you backbite and gossip about other people or spread wrong information about them, you do not* *really love them. Jesus Christ has given us the blueprint of how to resolve conflicts in Matthew 18:15–17. He said, if your brother trespasses against you, meet him first and tell him between you and him alone. If he does not listen, then take someone else with you. If he still does not listen, then tell the Church, and if he does not listen at this point, count him as a publican. Therefore, gossiping and backbiting under the guise of seeking ways to end a misunderstanding are not acceptable. It is not the way to love other people because you are pulling them down indirectly. Loving other people is keeping the bad things about them concealed as possible while magnifying the good about them.*

- **Making allowances for mistakes:** *Loving other people involves recognizing them as humans that are capable of making mistakes, and being gentle with them when they make such mistakes. We are all bound to do stupid things once in a while—not necessarily because we want to do those things, but because our knowledge is limited, and most of the times, we will act or react based on our limited understanding. If you expect other people to be perfect, you cannot love them. Ask yourself this same question, am I perfect? Many people excuse their imperfections, but magnify the shortcomings of other people! This is not the definition of loving others. In fact, loving other people means giving them the benefit of the doubt. You are always believing that they are doing everything with good intentions until you have proven them otherwise or beyond reasonable doubts. Even after* *you have discovered that they have other ulterior motives, you still have to love them — this is loving unconditionally!*

- **Sharing in their joys and sorrow:** *Some people find it easy to love sorrowful and hurting people. The challenge comes when the person moves from grief to joy, suddenly they become envious and jealous. True love is neither envious nor jealous. Loving other people truly means celebrating with them when they receive something that they have always wanted and weeping with them if something terrible happens to them. Romans 12:15 says, Rejoice with those who rejoice, and weep with those who weep. Irrespective of what you are going through, you must rejoice with those who rejoice and weep with those who weep. This is the way to love them!*

Loving other people is not always easy as it may seem because different people have different temperaments, background, and knowledge. For that reason, they behave in different ways of course. Some people are particularly difficult to love, while some others are easy to love. Nevertheless, I strongly believe that if we know why we should love them any how, it would become much easier for us to begin to show our love towards them.

The Rationale for Loving Other People

Our love for other people reflects the love of Christ for them: The effective way to convince a person that Jesus Christ loves him or her is by showing love. There is a limit to the kind of love that average human can demonstrate. When we go beyond the natural love and express supernatural love, it makes those who have not known Jesus Christ to be amazed. Thus, it is easier to tell them about His love for them. For example, if I go the extra mile in caring for other people, it is easier to say to them that Jesus Christ left His glory in heaven and came to earth to die for their sins. The LORD said emphatically that they will know that we are His disciples if we show them love. (See John 13:35). Therefore, if you want other people to know that you are a bonafide disciple of Jesus Christ, you must love them like He would have loved them Himself.

Loving other people shows that we love God: There is no better way to show our love for God than by loving other people. The Apostle John says, If anyone says, I love God, and yet hates his fellow Christian, he is a liar, because the one who does not love his fellow Christian whom he has seen cannot love God whom he has not seen (1 John 4:20). It is evident from this scriptural verse that anyone who does not love other people do not really love God.

Loving other people is a commandment: We must love other people because God commanded us to love them. Galatians 5:14 says, For the whole law can be summed up in a single commandment, namely, You must love your neighbor as yourself. If you are a Christian, the commandment of God for you is to love other people. One of the reasons we often find it challenging to love other people is that we often focus more on the people who are to receive our love rather than the One who commanded us to love them.

There is no commandment that God gives that is without its benefits, and loving other people is not left out. Here are some of the benefits of loving other people:

1. Increased desire for self-improvement: As you seek to demonstrate true love for other people, your human weaknesses will get in the way. However, your determination to love them will create a passion for dealing with those weaknesses. And by doing this, you are improving yourself. Let us look at the case of a father and a child for example: a father may have been extravagant with his spending habit before having a child, but once a child is born, he will have to adjust and learn how to spend wisely. He must change his spending habit because he knows that one of the ways to show his love for the child is by providing for his or her needs. Secondly, he must also learn how to shed other bad habits that may influence the child negatively. Although the father is simply trying to show his love for the child, he is at the same time becoming a better person. Always, when you show your love for other people, you grow to become a better person in the process.
2. Joy unfathomable: There is an indescribable joy that comes with obedience to God's Words or His commandments. When you love other people consistently,

you will find the joy of the LORD bubbling in your heart regardless of what circumstance you may be having physically in your own life. This joy is essential for your well-being as it is written in Proverbs 17:22: a cheerful heart brings good healing, but a crushed spirit dries up the bones. In fact, there is a joy that comes from seeing other people do well by showing them love. When a person who supposed to be mourning suddenly burst into laughter because of your act of love, you will also feel his or her joy.

3. Decreased anxiety and depression: Several people allow what other people do to get to them, and it can causes them anxiety and depression. However, when you love other people, you make room for their mistakes or errors. In such cases, you will not be all worked up when they do something you consider to be wrong. You will have peace of mind because you are not suspecting anyone. You simply think well of them instead of negatively. Those who cannot love other people are constantly afraid because of suspicion and lack of trust for anyone.

4. Relieved loneliness: Those who love other people improve themselves to a point where they are more relatable. Those who do not love others experience more loneliness because they cannot associate with people. In the same token, other people will find it difficult relating with them as well. This is why it is imperative that you love other people.

5. Increased productivity: Jesus Christ expects us to bring people to know Him — to welcome and receive Him. It will be challenging for anyone who does not love other people to bring anyone to the knowledge of Jesus Christ. On the other hand, those who engage in the practices of loving other people can bring them to experience Jesus Christ. They can influence more people because of their loving lifestyles and for the fact that they have greater opportunities to relate with others.

I want us to consider the reasons why some people find it difficult to love others. I believe that by knowing exactly what to do, we can overcome the challenges and begin to love other people better.

Why Is It Difficult to Love Other people?

- Misunderstanding of true love: Some of us think of love only as an emotion. The problem with this is that most of the times, our feelings are beyond our control. While we can control how we react to our emotions, the emotions themselves just happen. So when we do not feel love emotions toward a person, we conclude that we cannot love him or her. True love is more than feelings — it involves a decision. Jesus did not feel like being crucified and dying on the cross. He prayed in Gethsemane that the cup might pass over Him, however, He still gave Himself to die for our sins because He loves us. Therefore, we cannot base our love for other people on emotions. If we do, we will only love a few people, at best!

- Relying on our strength: Many times we try to love other people by the power of our will. When we discover that we have problems loving them, we try to figure out all the psychological and physical reasons behind that. Although it might not be wrong to do this, we must know that only God by His Holy Spirit can help us to love other people effectively. Therefore, we must submit ourselves to Him and rely on the characters and abilities that His Holy Spirit supplies.

- Our humanity: As humans, there are those we flow naturally with, and there are those we cannot flow with, but God commands us to love them all. There is no discrimination in love! We often find it difficult to love those who do not flow with us. We may not flow with them for different reasons: their temperaments or ways of doing things, but we must love them regardless. We cannot wait for a person to be lovable before we can love him or her. Truthfully speaking, Jesus did not wait for us to be lovable before dying for our sins on the cross.

- Fear of getting hurt: Many Christians do not love other people because they are afraid of being hurt. Some of us are afraid of bearing the pain of rejection after reaching out in love to other people. This is very important, we must know that for us to be made perfect in love, we must let go our fears. We have to always remember that we are living in a fallen world, and people have different experiences that influence their behaviors at different times. Therefore, we must exercise caution not to expect everyone to always reciprocate our acts of love. As Christians, empowered by the love of Jesus Christ, we are to show love for other people consistently.

- Selfishness: Some Christians only think about themselves — their conveniences, successes, well-beings, and so forth. Such people cannot love others because loving other people means putting them into consideration when you are planning your own life. A selfish and self-centered person will find it difficult to share his or her goods with other people except when there is a potential benefit of getting something back from them. Such individual only gives to the rich because the rich is in the position to reciprocate. Selfishness will never allow us to effectively love other people!

- Pride: This is arguably the most significant reason why we find it difficult to love other people. Many of us are too proud to serve others, especially those who seem to be below us when it comes to achieving material possessions. Some people do not like to associate with people who are not in their social clique. It is more saddening that there are Christians who cannot love another Christian from a different denomination. Pride of race, face, achievements, and possessions will hinder us from demonstrating genuine love for other people.

How to Practice True Love for Other People

Until we know how to demonstrate true love for other people we may end-up doing less or exceeding what love would have demanded from us. Some people will not tell others the truth about themselves — their characters for example because they think love does not rebuke or correct. They think love only pampers people and accepts all their offenses and faults. They misunderstand accepting people the way they are for taking all their flaws without pointing them to their attentions. The question is how then could they improve themselves without correction? Pointing out your flaws and shortcomings will give you the chance to correct and improve yourself. Now, let us discuss in more details how to love other people effectively:

1. Get to know other people: Sometimes, the reason people do not appreciate our acts of love is that, we do not take enough time to learn and understand what their needs are before taking action. Imagine giving a drawing board to a student who is in dire need of a graph book. It is important to try to know a person before doing anything that we consider to be an act of love towards him or her. Knowing him or her does not simply mean to know all about the fine details of about his or her live, rather to know whether what you want to give is really what he or she needs. One of the easiest

ways to get to know people is to spend time with them. When you spend time with a person, he or she may end-up exposing and sharing his or her needs without even realizing it. Another way to get to know people is to observe them. If a person has been wearing the same pair of jeans for weeks, you may consider getting him or her another pair of jeans. If his or her shoes are worn out, you may consider getting him or her a new boot. There is no way you can get to know these needs if you are not observant. Set your mind daily to be a blessing to other people. Let it be in your subconscious that you are interested in knowing what other people need and how you can be of a help. Sometimes, it is by facial expressions and outward looks that you are able to discern. If a person has always been cheerful and lively, but one day he or she is sullen and withdrawn, you should call him or her aside and ask questions. These are some of the ways we can get to know other people and their respective needs.

2. Accept people: We are all aware that we are different in many unique ways. This difference may be because of our family background, educational background, exposure, race, city, location, and numerous other factors. If we must genuinely love other people, we must celebrate our differences. When we talk about differences, we do not mean celebrating iniquities, sins, transgressions and trespasses instead, we are to celebrate our differences in thoughts, actions, and understanding,

etc. If you love chocolates and you want to love a person who hates chocolates, you would not talk about chocolates every time you are together. You have to accept the fact that when it comes to eating chocolates, the two of you are different. You must avoid criticizing other people for who they are! Learn to love them the way they are, and do good to them the way they will appreciate it.

3. Overlook offenses as much as possible: I have stated previously that one of the ways to get to know other people is by spending more time with them. One way or another, there is going to be an opportunity for someone to offend you. Some people may even hurt you deliberately, and sometimes, you will feel offended by different individuals. You must carefully think the offenses through before reacting. Some offenses are light and may not need any confrontation or escalation. If a person accidentally steps on your toes, you do not have to act in anger or rage. Nevertheless, there are significant offenses that may demand for confrontation. For example, if a person made up a story about your spouse having affairs, you should have a serious conversation with that individual. One of the things I have noticed about people is that if you always complain about minor errors, they may not take you seriously even when you are addressing a major problem. On the other hand, if you always let the minor issues

pass, they will take you seriously when you approach them with considerable matters.

4. Be assertive in communication: Many Christians misunderstand loving other people to mean that you endure the wrongs without ever saying anything. They expect you to bear everything and remain patient. The truth is that you must always help people to grow by showing them their errors. Assertive communication involves giving other people the benefit of the doubt: call a private meeting between you and them. You need to allow them the opportunity to express and defend themselves. Listen to them without any bias and try as much as possible to understand everything they have to say. Help them to become better by instructing them how they could handled the situation better. If we look at the early Church in Acts 6, the problem was that some people were left out of the daily provision of food. The Christians did not say, "Oh, because we are to love other people, we will not say or do anything about the situation." Instead, they spoke to the relevant authority, detailing the problem precisely. They were also attentive as the other party attempted to provide a solution to the problem, and the issue was resolved amicably. Sometimes, when we fail to communicate assertively, we hurt ourselves, and eventually our love for other people is affected.

5. Be truthful: I want to relate this part to our previous point of speaking assertively. If someone is walking in

error, you must not shy away, but communicate with the individual concerning the issues. The Apostle Paul had to do this with the Apostle Peter. Let us look at Galatians 2:11–14, But when Cephas came to Antioch, I opposed him to his face, because he had clearly done wrong. Until certain people came from James, he had been eating with the Gentiles. But when they arrived, he stopped doing this and separated himself because he was afraid of those who were pro-circumcision. And the rest of the Jews also joined with him in this hypocrisy, so that even Barnabas was led astray with them by their hypocrisy. But when I saw that they were not behaving consistently with the truth of the gospel, I said to Cephas in front of them all, If you, although you are a Jew, live like a Gentile and not like a Jew, how can you try to force the Gentiles to live like Jews? Paul clearly showed us that one of the ways to love other people is to show them the errors of their ways, especially if it relates to God's commandments.

6. Pray: Sometimes, you may find it difficult to begin to love other people until you start to pray for them. When you give your time to pray for a person, you help release them from the grip of the satanic powers. You move the Holy Spirit to touch and flood their hearts with light, and you help them to become the kind of person God wants them to be. By so doing, it will become easy for them to receive your love towards them. Prayer also helps you to speak less about the offenses

and faults of other people. It helps you to avoid getting angry because a person does not appreciate your display of love yet. You just have the conviction and confidence within your heart that you have prayed for them and change will begin to affect their lives. Furthermore, when you pray for other people, God will begin to give you more grace to love them even better.

Loving others is an act of obedience to God that has several benefits so, you do not want to miss out on those benefits because of pride and selfishness. Begin to practice genuine, sincere, and godly love for other people today!

"Forgiveness removes any walls between you and God. Forgiveness is vertical as well as horizontal. Let us say it the other way around: Unforgiveness toward a human being also blocks your fellowship with God."

Myles Monroe

NOTE

VICTOR HICKSON SR

FORGIVENESS

W   ɔhasiz-
is that
essen-
tial ing   veness
is amaz   e of or
detox fı   you to
love otl   neigh-
bors. Your neighbors are not basically your family members or loved ones, but generally everyone. As with love, forgiveness is often misunderstood and misrepresented. Henceforth, this chapter will be devoted to exposing the proper perspective to forgiveness. We will be focusing mainly on what forgiveness means and what it does not mean. We will also delve into the unique benefits of forgiving people and how to gauge the truthfulness or sincerity of your forgiveness.

What Does Forgiveness Mean?

• 65 •

Forgiveness is a decision to sacrificially relinquish your right not to punish or avenge a person who has faulted or offended you in any way. In other words, forgiveness is not necessarily an emotional expression or feeling. It is an action or reaction you take consciously in obedience to God; therefore, you need His grace to forgive others. Forgiveness means instead of excommunicating or pushing a person away because of his/her offense or fault, you choose to retain the individual rather than retaliating and reprimanding him or her for the offense or fault.

Now, you have to see why forgiveness is sacrificial! Remember that God had to sacrifice His only begotten Son to forgive our sins. So, we have to sacrifice our anger and pride to forgive others. Forgiveness is accepting pain and hurt from past and present incidents and choosing to move on with life knowing that you cannot undo or change what has happened. It is showing the willingness to let go momentary pleasure of erecting a wall of resentment and bitterness against anyone who has done you wrong. Furthermore, forgiveness is sacrificing the possibility of retaliating now or in the future. It is choosing never to blackmail, intimidate, antagonize, backbite or gossip about the issue any longer!

Forgiveness is choosing to trust that "all things work together for good to them that love God, to them who are called according to his purpose" (Romans 8:28). It is a commitment to believing in the goodness of God and therefore releasing an offender to go free. To forgive others is to prove to God that He did not send His Son to die in vain for you. It also demonstrates that the power of His Holy Spirit is effectively working in your life.

Forgiveness is a decision to grow above the pains and hurts inflicted upon you through the actions or inaction of the offender. It is choosing to become better at relating with others by doing good to them rather than repaying them for the evil they have done against you. Please understand that it is not becoming neutral to the offender, but rather actively doing good to the individual.

Misrepresentations of Forgiveness

1. Pretending that the offense or fault never happen: Forgiving an offender or someone who committed a fault against you is not the same as pretending that the incident never occurred. Forgiveness is not an act of deception. To sincerely forgive, there must be an acknowledgment that an offense or fault has been committed. And because of the incident, your life has been affected negatively. Forgiveness is saying, even though I am offended or deeply hurt as a result of your actions, I choose to show my love for you by forgiving you.

2. Condoning the offense or fault: regardless of the nature of the offense or fault, you have to forgive — sometimes, even those whom you have forgiven will have to deal with certain consequences for their actions. In 2 Samuel 12:9–13, we see that God forgave David of his sins of murder and adultery, and yet he had to deal

with the consequences of those sinful behaviors. I want you to know that the LORD allowed David's acts of sin to be recorded for us to read today. As Christians, we must never condone sin, iniquity, transgressions and trespasses. When someone's behavior(s) or action(s) offend us, we must endeavor to let him or her know politely — out of love and caring that his or her action is wrong. Most importantly, we must always be prepared to forgive the individual. The Bible said, Those who call evil good and good evil are as good as dead, who turn darkness into light and light into darkness, who turn bitter into sweet and sweet into bitter (Isaiah 5:20). Therefore, we should never excuse unrighteousness!

3. Allowing people to take advantage of you: Some people's views of forgiveness can turn them foolish. For instance, a person borrows a sum of money for a specific purpose, but instead of using the money for the intended purpose, he/she simply squander the money on other things. The borrower then returns to apologize and ask for more money to borrow. That view lacks proper representation of what forgiveness really mean. It is simply acting foolishly! To be fair, it is a general rule not to loan money to those who will not put it to profitable use! By not using the money profitably, the borrower may not be able to repay the loan. Forgiveness, in such a case would means to either forfeit or cancel the entire debt or loan amount if you are willing and able to do so. You must avoid harboring resentment or

bitterness toward the person! You have to know that you are not under any obligation to keep lending money to such an individual. At best, if you think that such person is genuinely sorry or has changed his ways, you may proceed with giving him or her less amount to prove him or herself by doing something profitable before extending larger loan amount again. It is also essential not to write the person off entirely because people do change. Nevertheless, what is foolish is to believe that he or she has changed without proving him or her.

4. Pardoning without any valid justification: God does not forgive those who do not repent and turn away from their wickedness. He does not command us to forgive those He has not forgiven. When people continue to do evil, God can bring judgment upon them according to their works. Forgiveness does not mean extending the hands of fellowship to a person who has not turned from his or her wicked ways. For example, if a man sexually harasses a woman and refuses to repent, it would be foolish for the woman to relate closely to the man. The Bible encourages us "not be angry and frustrated" when you are a victim of cruel mistreatment and the person refuses to repent. Do not fret! That only leads to trouble! (Psalm 37:8). You might choose not to take revenge, however, you must take the proper steps to secure every channel through which the person may use to do you wrong again.

5. Placing the blames on others or passing the buck: Some people think that forgiveness is about overlooking every pain and hurt or just suppressing your feeling by concluding that it is all the other party's fault. Sometimes you may need to take the blame for being too quick to take offense. You may need to sit back and ask yourself if you deserve to be angry because of the actions or reactions of the other person. The Bible warns us, Do not let yourself be quickly provoked, for anger resides in the lap of fools (Ecclesiastes 7:9). Therefore, you should allow yourself some time to grow to a point where any and everything will no longer provokes you easily. If you always place the blame on someone else or pass the buck, you will deny yourself the opportunity to grow.

6. Forgetting: there are those who think that forgiveness is the same as forgetting that an offense happened. This is self-deception, and it is psychologically impossible to forget that someone offended you within a short period. It takes years to forget sometimes depending on the nature of the offense. For example, you can expect a person who had a coffee spilled on his shirt to forget within a few days. On the other hand, a teenage girl who was sexually harassed by anyone may not forget the incident for the rest of her life. Forgiveness is not the same word with forgetting something, even though forgiveness can lead us to forget after we have forgiven. True forgiveness is letting go the feeling of

resentment and bitterness that suddenly arises when you come into contact or proximity with the person who has offended you.

7. Not feeling the pain any longer: Forgiveness does not mean that you will no longer feel any pain and hurt because of the offense or fault. Instead, it means not allowing the pain and hurt to affect your interaction with the offender. Forgiveness means that the pain and hurt of the offense does not cause you to become touchy or to seek for retaliation. We are emotional beings, and our emotions are sometimes not controllable. However, we can control how we react when we are emotionally provoked. This is what forgiveness brings into our lives when we learn to forgive others!

Always, forgiveness takes process. Yes, the decision to forgive may begin at some point, but the demonstration of that decision is a process. Sometimes you have to remind yourself that you have forgiven this person when you see him or her. Some other times, you may have to speak out loudly that you love him or her.

Benefits of Practicing Forgiveness

- You receive forgiveness by forgiving: Jesus says, If you forgive others their sins, your heavenly Father will also forgive you. But if you do not forgive others, your Father will not forgive you your sins (Matthew 6:14–15).

It is evident that forgiving others is the key to receiving forgiveness from God. Unforgiveness is a sin, and if you do not repent and forgive others, you cannot be forgiven. You should consider one simple fact: if God can forgive you of all your sins, you must likewise forgive those who offended or faulted you.

- You must learn to move from the past: Unforgiveness keeps you stuck in the past: it prevents you from moving forward. When you hold resentment or bitterness in your heart against someone, you will spend most of your time thinking negatively about that person. The truth is that the other person is moving on with his or her life, while you are stuck in the thoughts of the past. This will hinder your spiritual and physical progression. When you forgive — and let go of resentments and bitterness, you will begin to think more positively and make room for greater productivity. You will start to grow stronger!

- You become more compassionate: Forgiving others helps you to become more compassionate. It takes compassion to truly forgive! Act of forgiveness brings us into higher levels of empathy. It allows for you to think of the offender in a better light — to see the reasons for his or her actions. Forgiving others helps you to perceive people more clearly rather than focusing only on their wrongs.

- Sustained relationships: Many people cannot maintain their relationships with their spouses, children, friends,

family members, and others because of their unwilling-
ness to forgive. There is no way to relate with people
long-term without being offended. I have stated earlier that most people will not deliberately hurt or cause
you pain, however, it is not to say that they will never
offend you at some point. Nevertheless, if you choose
to forgive them, you will sustain the relationships longer. Forgiveness will make others to want to relate with
you because they will not be over-cautious about stepping on land mines. In other words, most people pre-
fer to associate with people who forgives rather than
those who are unwilling to forgive.

- Health benefits: Forgiveness is associated with several
  health benefits: they include but not limited to lower
  blood pressure, stress reduction, better anger manage-
  ment, decreased risk of alcohol and substance abuse,
  lesser depression and anxiety syndromes, better psychological well-being, and many others.

Christians are to forgive others because God has forgiven
them through Jesus Christ. The Apostle Paul wrote, Instead,
be kind to one another, compassionate, forgiving one another, just as God in Christ also forgave you (Ephesians 4:31). In
other words, forgiving others is one of the best ways to show
God that we appreciate what He did for us — giving His only
begotten Son to die for our sins on the cross when we do not
deserve it. Another part is that Christians are to forgive others

as an instruction from the LORD. Forgiveness shows the world that we are disciples of Jesus Christ.

There are two sets of people that you must forgive to move forward in life: 1) is yourself and 2) is other people. Some people's problems are because of lack of self-forgiveness! They can forgive everyone else but they don't know how to forgive themselves. So, you have to understand how to forgive yourself and how to forgive other people around your life.

How to Forgive Yourself

1. Admit your wrongdoing: If you are always placing the blame on others or passing the buck, you will find it difficult to forgive yourself when you finally realize that you are the guilty one. The very first step to forgiving yourself is to come to realization that you are capable of doing wrong. Wrong here does not necessarily mean falling into sin. You can make simple mistakes like anyone else. Because you are human with limited knowledge and understanding, you are going to make mistakes sometimes. Do not feel ashamed of your mistakes — simply admit them. Accept your fault and move on to the next stage.

2. Apologize to those you have offended or faulted: The next step to forgiving yourself is to apologize to those who feel offended as a result of your actions or inaction. First, repent and turn to the LORD concerning the situation or event, if you think He is affected by what

you have done. Secondly, apologize to the individual that is affected by your action or behavior. Some people only repent unto the LORD but never apologize to those they have offended or faulted. In such scenarios, you will not truly forgive yourself because you will always feel bad when those people accuse you of hurting them. You have to apologize to anyone who is hurt by your actions regardless of their age, social status or relationship. Please be extremely sensitive not to add the elements of pride and self-justification to your apology. Let them know that you whole-heartedly admit what you have done wrong, and you are genuinely sorry. Finally, commit yourself to doing everything in your power to avoid repeating such mistakes in the future.

3. Let go of the negative thoughts and emotions: It is inevitable that when you admit your offenses or faults, you will feel negative about yourself. However, you have to let go of those negative thoughts and emotions. You must begin to learn that those wrong deeds are not who you are. In fact, they do not define your identity! Your life is defined in Christ according to Scriptures. You are forgiven and accepted in the Beloved! Re-emphasize to yourself the fact that you have repented and apologized, and doing everything you can possibly do to avoid repeating the same wrongs again. Never allow the enemy to guilt-trip you, and do not let anyone use emotional blackmail on you. Some people would

want to remind you of the offense or fault continually. Therefore, every time they remind you, bring back to your attention that you have been forgiven, and simply, overlook them. Do not try to argue with them because they will continue to raise the same topic every other time. Once they see that you are not moved by the emotional blackmails, they will cease to bring it up.

4. Learn from your mistakes: There are no points going through all the steps outlined above if you are going to remain doing the same wrong things over and over again. Besides admitting your wrong, you must put some structures in place to help you from doing the same wrong things.

How to Forgive Others

- Acknowledge that you are offended and hurt: As I mentioned earlier, forgiveness is not self-deception! In a better term, forgiveness is not pretending as if nothing has happened. The very first step to forgiving others is to accept that you are in pain — deeply hurt because of someone's action or behavior. If you do not know what they did that hurt you, how then will you address the issue precisely. Think about the incident that led to your hurt so you are sure of what the other person did that made you to feel hurt.

- Decide to forgive those who offended or committed fault against you: As soon as you become aware of your

pain and hurt, you must take a step to forgive your offender. The reason you must think things over is to exercise diligent caution to understand the basis of your
forgiveness. You need more than a motivation — you
need the grace of God to convert your decision into
action. You can look at the fact that the LORD also forgave you of your wrongs. You can look at the need to
keep your relationship with the individual. You can also
look at other strong or compelling reasons to keep you
away from backing out of the processes of forgiving.

- Do not hide your feelings toward those who offend or
  committed fault against you: The next practical step to
  take in forgiving a person is to tell him or her that you
  are affected and painfully hurt by what they did. Do not
  worry about whether the person will or will not admit
  any wrong. In cultivating an environment and atmosphere of resolution, you must be careful not to guilt-
  trip the person when telling him or her about how you
  feel. You have to be assertive with saying exactly what
  the individual did that hurt your feelings.

- Stop thinking about the offense or fault: inasmuch
  you continue to think about the offense or fault, you
  will keep on releasing negative emotions. By restrain-
  ing the thoughts, you will start to mute the negative
  emotions. It is very possible that sometimes, you may
  unconsciously or sub-consciously begin to think about
  the offense or fault again. You want to immediately
  take control of the thought once you become aware.

This is something that happens on-and-off. You do not have to beat yourself down for thinking about the situation or event.

- Take action to forgive: It's now time to turn your decision into positive action. Depending on the response of the offender and the nature of the offense or fault, take the step to restore the relationship and offer the individual the right hand of friendship again!

Always remember that forgiveness gives you more benefits than the person who receives forgiveness. Therefore, begin to engage practically in forgiving people around you.

Conclusion

As Christians, we are supposed to allow for the love of God to affect and influence our lives more and more both in loving God, loving ourselves, and loving other people! Finally, we are to practice forgiving others. I believe you have learned in this book how to love better!

One more thing, I want to give you a piece of advice: until you do something with what you have read or learned, nothing will really change. You may not become perfect automatically so give yourself some time to grow as you engage in the practices of loving both spiritually and physically. Soon or later, you will begin to be made perfect in love!

BIBLIOGRAPHY

Spurgeon, Charles. Spurgeon on Prayer & Spiritual Warfare. New Kensington, PA: Whitaker House, 1998.

Sumrall, Lester. Angels to Help You. New Kensington, PA: Whitaker House, 1999.

Pioneers of Faith. Tulsa, OK: Harrison House, 1995.

Tari, Mel. Like a Mighty Wind. Carol Stream, IL: Creation House, 1971.

The Gentle Breeze of Jesus. Carol Stream, IL: Creation House, 1974.

Tenney, Tommy. The God Chasers. Shippensburg, PA: Destiny Image Publishers, 1998.

Torrey, R. A. How to Obtain Fullness of Power. New Kensington, PA: Whitaker House, 1984.

Unger, Merrill F. Demons in the World Today. Wheaton, IL: Tyndale House Publishers, 1971.

Walters, Kathie. Celtic Flames. Macon, GA: Good News Ministries, 1999.

Columba: The Celtic Dove. Macon, GA: Good News Ministries, 1999.

Ward Heflin, Ruth. Glory. Hagerstown, MD: McDougal Publishing Company, 1990.

Golden Glory. Hagerstown, MD: McDougal Publishing Company, 2000.

Harvest Glory: I Ask for the Nations. Hagerstown, MD: Mc-Dougal Publishing Company, 1999.

Unifying Glory. Hagerstown, MD: McDougal Publishing Company, 2000.

Wigglesworth, Smith, and Wayne E. Warner. The Anointing of His Spirit. Ann Arbor, MI: Vine Books, 1994.

Ever Increasing Faith. New Kensington, PA: Whitaker House, 2000.

Smith Wigglesworth on Healing. New Kensington, PA: Whitaker House, 1999.

Smith Wigglesworth on Power to Serve. New Kensington, PA: Whitaker House, 1998.

Woodworth-Etter, Maria, and Larry Keefauver. The Original Maria Woodworth-Etter Devotional. Orlando, FL: Creation House, 1997.

A Diary of Signs & Wonders. Tulsa, OK: Harrison House, 1980.

The Holy Spirit. New Kensington, PA: Whitaker House, 1998

ABOUT THE AUTHOR

At the age of twelve, Pastor Victor Hickson learned first-hand about the awesome working of the power of God when he was healed of a heart condition. In a separate account, God protected him from bleeding to death after he was viciously attacked by two dogs. Pastor Victor Hickson, received the calling of God at the age of thirty and was ordained as a Minister of the gospel. God opened the door in 1991, and he became the Pastor of Triumphant Church of God in Christ where he served faithfully for seven years.

In December of 1999, God gave Pastor Victor Hickson a vision for Full Deliverance Ministry. God began to opened several doors for his ministry: from renting to partnering with other Church Organizations, and eventually, relocating to the far south. In January of 2009, after forty seven years, Pastor Victor Hickson became the first African-American Pastor of First Baptist Church of Florida City. In January of 2010, Changing Your Direction Television Broadcast was launched – reaching over twenty million viewers. Changing Your Direction Television Broadcast is seen both locally on Comcast and nationally on Aspire Network.

Pastor Victor Hickson received honorary degree from Jackson Baptist Theological Seminary and has made several Guest appearances on such Christian Television Networks as

Trinity Broadcasting Network. Pastor Victor Hickson oversees one of the fastest growing Churches in South Florida today with a Charter School that has over four hundred students – serving from kindergarten through the eighth grade. The Ministry has also a free health clinic serving over five thousand patients a year, and host many other ministries. Our Ministry Food Drive Program currently feeds one thousand families monthly. Pastor Victor Hickson trusted faithfully in the vision that God had given him, and today, he is seeing the ministry grow spiritually and physically as many lives are being impacted by the saving, healing and deliverance power of God.

The goal of Our Ministry is to build the Kingdom of Jesus Christ in the hearts and minds of the people by the power of the Holy Spirit. We believe that a little become much when you place it in the Master's hand!

CONTACT THE AUTHOR

For more information about Victor Hickson, Sr., or to contact the author for worldwide speaking engagements visit:

Website: www.changingyourdirection.org

Email: rev.VictorHickson@gmail.com

Or call: 305.283.6817

VICTOR HICKSON SR

LOVING BETTER

VICTOR HICKSON SR

LOVING BETTER

CPSIA information can be obtained
at www.ICGtesting.com
Printed in the USA
LVHW011809030422
715134LV00001B/3

9 781087 882055